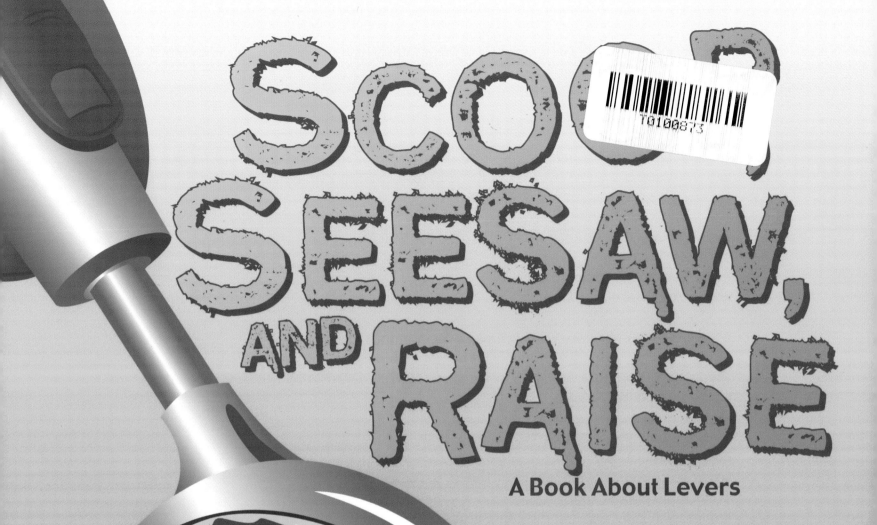

SCOOP, SEESAW, AND RAISE

A Book About Levers

by Michael Dahl

illustrated by Denise Shea

Special thanks to our advisers for their expertise:

Youwen Xu, Professor
Department of Physics and Astronomy
Minnesota State University, Mankato, MN

Susan Kesselring, M.A.
Literacy Educator
Rosemount–Apple Valley–Eagan (Minnesota) School District

PICTURE WINDOW BOOKS
Minneapolis, Minnesota

Editor: Jacqueline Wolfe
Designer: Joseph Anderson
Page Production: Joseph Anderson
Creative Director: Keith Griffin
Editorial Director: Carol Jones
The illustrations in this book were created digitally.

Picture Window Books
1710 Roe Crest Drive
North Mankato, Minnesota 56003
www.picturewindowbooks.com

Library of Congress Cataloging-in-Publication Data
Dahl, Michael.
Scoop, seesaw, and raise : a book about levers / by Michael Dahl ; illustrated by Denise Shea.
 p. cm. — (Amazing science)
Includes bibliographical references and index.
ISBN-13: 978-1-4048-1303-8 (hardcover)
ISBN-10: 1-4048-1303-9 (hardcover)
ISBN-13: 978-1-4048-1910-8 (paperback)
ISBN-10: 1-4048-1910-X (paperback)
1. Levers—Juvenile literature. I. Shea, Denise. II. Title. III. Series.
TJ147.D3245 2005
621.8'11—dc22   2005024973

TABLE OF CONTENTS

Painting a garage is hard, hot, sweaty work.

It's time for a break. A metal opener pops off the top of a soda pop can. Ahhhhh!

Did you know that all day you have been working with simple machines called levers?

WHAT IS A LEVER?

A simple machine is any tool or device that helps us work. A simple machine does not always have an engine or buttons or make loud noises.

A lever is a simple machine made of a stiff bar that rests on a fulcrum. The bar is the part of the lever that moves up or down. The fulcrum does not move. This machine is so simple that many times we use a lever without knowing it.

When you opened the soda pop can, you used a lever.

BAR

FULCRUM

HOW A LEVER WORKS

When you use a screwdriver to open a can of paint, you are using another lever. The long metal body of the screwdriver is the bar of the lever. The part of the screwdriver that rests against the can and does not move is the fulcrum.

Push down on the handle of the screwdriver and the other end moves up. Snap! The lid pops open.

A SEESAW IS A LEVER

Watch children play on a seesaw, or teeter-totter.

When a child sits down on one seat of the seesaw, she is using force, or effort. The seesaw gives her extra force to lift the friend at the other end. Without the lever's special help, she could not lift her friend by herself.

SCOOP

An ice-cream scoop works the same way. Effort is applied to one end of the scoop by your hand. The other end lifts a scoop of delicious ice cream. The fulcrum is in the middle of the ice-cream scoop, where your fingers grip the handle.

Another lever on the playground is a digger, or scoop. One end of the metal bar is pulled down. The other end scoops up sand or dirt. The digger is a first-class lever like a seesaw.

13

BOTTLE OPENER

The bottle opener works like another type of lever. This time the fulcrum is not in the middle of the bar. The fulcrum is at the end.

ROOT BEER

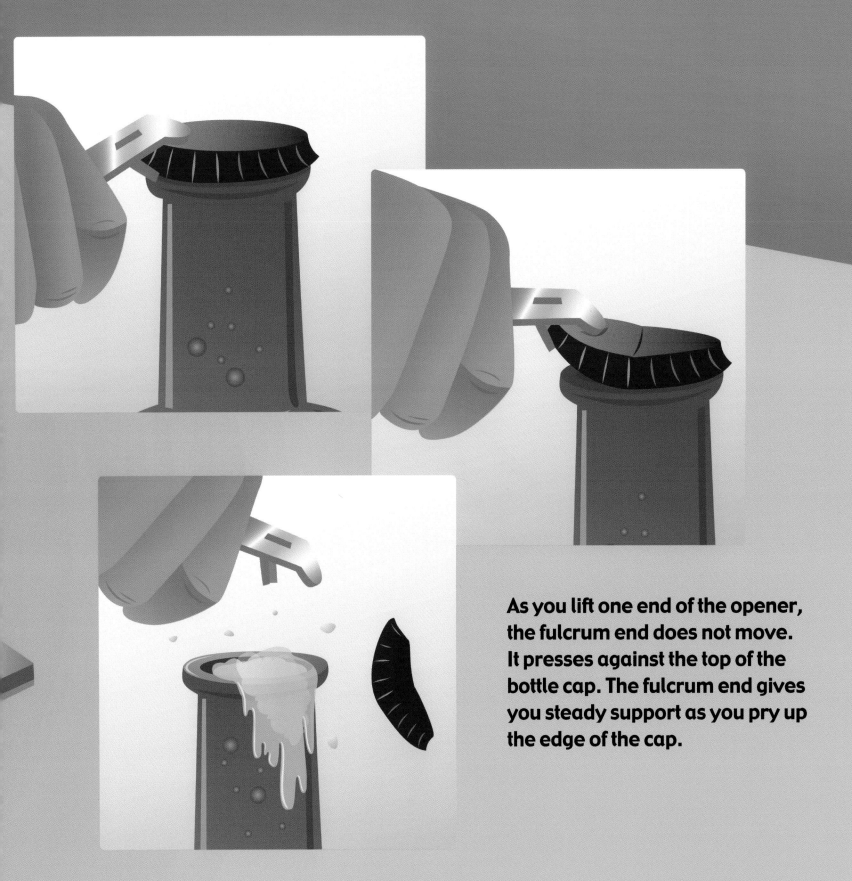

As you lift one end of the opener, the fulcrum end does not move. It presses against the top of the bottle cap. The fulcrum end gives you steady support as you pry up the edge of the cap.

BROOMS AND BRUSHES

A broom is a third kind of lever. The broom sweeps back and forth. Its bristles collect dirt and dust.

The broom's fulcrum is near the top where your hand grips the broomstick. The effort is made in the middle, where your other hand moves the stick back and forth. The load is the other end where the bristles sweep the dirt. This kind of lever is called a third-class lever.

Paintbrushes are also third-class levers. They sweep up and down against the wall. Their soft bristles splash paint against the flat surface. Brushes and brooms are simple machines that help us clean and make things look brand new.

FIRST-, SECOND-, AND THIRD CLASS LEVERS

Every day we use all three kinds of levers to help us work. The class of a lever simply tells us where the fulcrum rests, and where the effort is made.

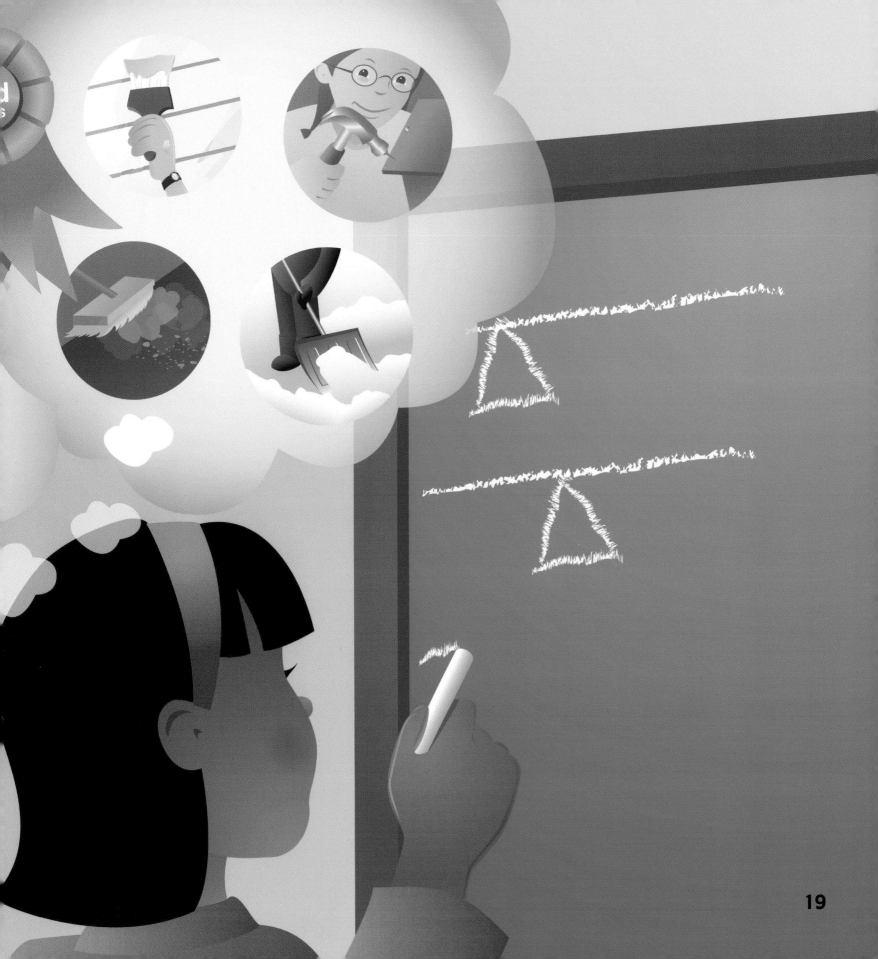

FUN LEVERS

Not all levers help us work. Some levers, like these hockey sticks, help us play. The hockey sticks help move the hockey puck across the ice. How do you use levers to work and play?

MARSHMALLOW MADNESS: HOW A LEVER WORKS

MATERIALS:
- Large marshmallow
- Unsharpened pencil
- Ruler
- Yard stick
- Adult

WHAT YOU DO:
1. Lay the pencil down on a table. Put the ruler across the pencil so it looks like a mini seesaw.
2. Ask an adult to stand the yardstick on end with the zero mark on the table.
3. Line the 2 inch (5 cm) mark of the ruler up with the pencil. Place the marshmallow on the end of the ruler farthest away from the pencil.
4. Hit the short end of the ruler with your hand, shooting the marshmallow into the air. Watch closely as it flies up and measure how high up it goes on the yard stick.
5. Next, move the ruler so the pencil lines up with the 2 inch (5 cm) mark. Repeat step 4.
6. Repeat Step 4 at the 4, 6, and 8 inch (10, 15, 20 cm) marks on the ruler.
7. Notice how the height the marshmallow flies in the air changes depending on where the pencil (or fulcrum) lines up with the ruler.

FOLLOW UP QUESTIONS:
1. What do you think would happen if you used something longer than a yard stick to propel the marshmallow?
2. What do you think would happen if you used something heavier than a marshmallow?

FUN FACTS

Fulcrum is pronounced FULL-krum. It means a strong, steady support.

The seesaw is called a first-class lever. First-class levers have their fulcrum in the center of the bar.

A lever only works when a human worker applies force, or effort, to the bar of the lever. The lever adds power to the worker's effort. Levers help workers move loads or open objects that are too difficult to move or open by hand.

A bottle opener is a second-class lever. Second-class levers have their fulcrum at one end, and a worker at the other end makes the effort. Another kind of second-class lever is a wheelbarrow.

GLOSSARY

First-class lever—a lever where the fulcrum rests in the middle of the bar
force—a power that can cause something else to move or change
fulcrum—the part of a lever that the bar rests on; it doesn't move
lever—a simple machine that helps do work; it has a fulcrum and bar
second-class lever—a lever where the fulcrum rests on one end of the bar
    and the effort is made on the other end
third-class lever—a lever where they effort is made in the middle of the bar,
    such as a broom or a paintbrush

TO LEARN MORE

AT THE LIBRARY

Douglas, Lloyd G. *What Is a Lever?* New York: Childrens's Press, 2002.

Fowler, Allan. *Simple Machines.* New York: Children's Press, 2001.

Frost, Helen & Gail Saunders-Smith. *What Are Levers (Looking at Simple Machines).* Mankato, Minn.: Pebble Books, 2001.

Wells, Robert E. *How Do You Lift a Lion?* Morton Grove, Ill.: Albert Whitman & Company, 1996.

INDEX

ON THE WEB

FactHound offers a safe, fun way to find Internet sites related to this book. All of the sites on FactHound have been researched by our staff.

1. Visit *www.facthound.com*
2. Type in this special code for age-appropriate sites: *1404813039*
3. Click on the FETCH IT button.

Your trusty FactHound will fetch the best sites for you!

LOOK FOR ALL THE BOOKS IN THE AMAZING SCIENCE SERIES: